Bike Riding Ace

By Micheline Grace
Illustrated by Kevin Purcell

Bike Riding Ace

Copyright © 2009 Micheline Grace and Kevin Purcell

All rights reserved.

ISBN: 1-4392-5373-0

Library of Congress number: 2009912338
Printed in Charleston, South Carolina

Contact Micheline at Micheline@gozindas.com for news on the "Neighborhood Series"!

To my sister, Julie...
because we always dreamed of having our own bikes.

Today is my birthday
Mom has a surprise
That she says I can have
If I cover my eyes.

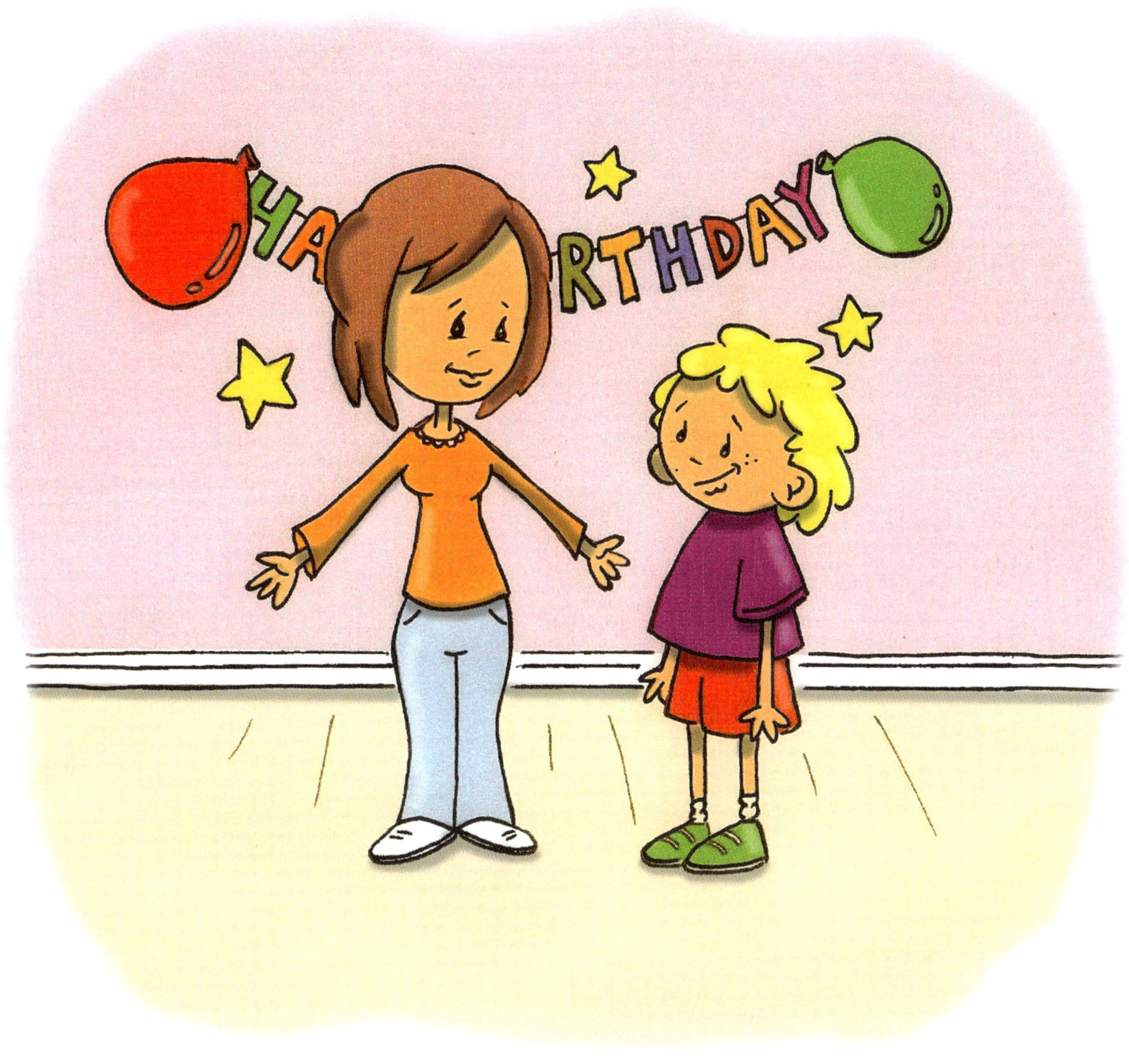
HA
RTHDAY

With her hands on my shoulders
We go out the back door
While I walk very carefully
Since I can't see the floor.

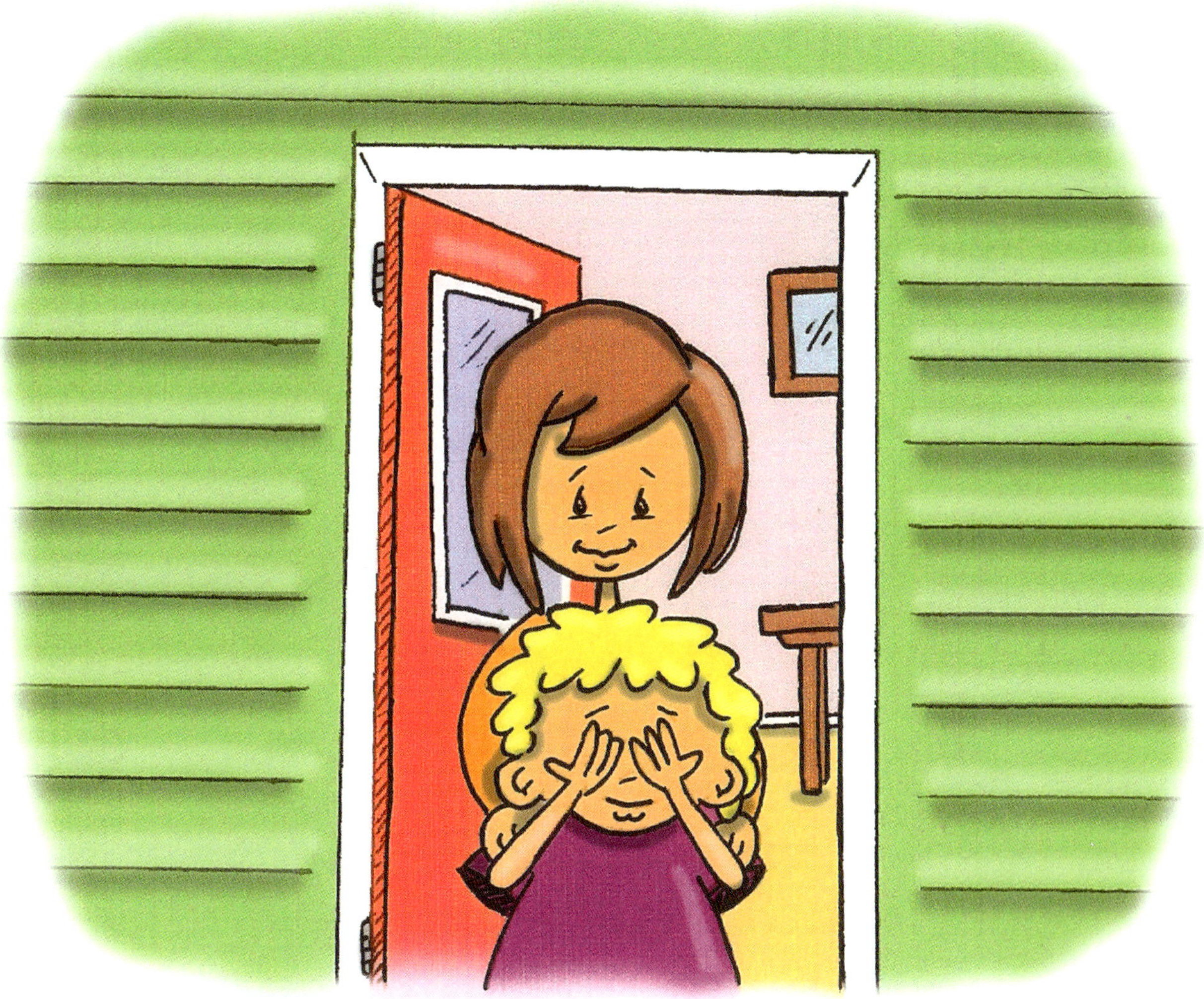

"OK, you can look"
My mom says to me sweetly
So I lower my hands
While my whole family greets me.

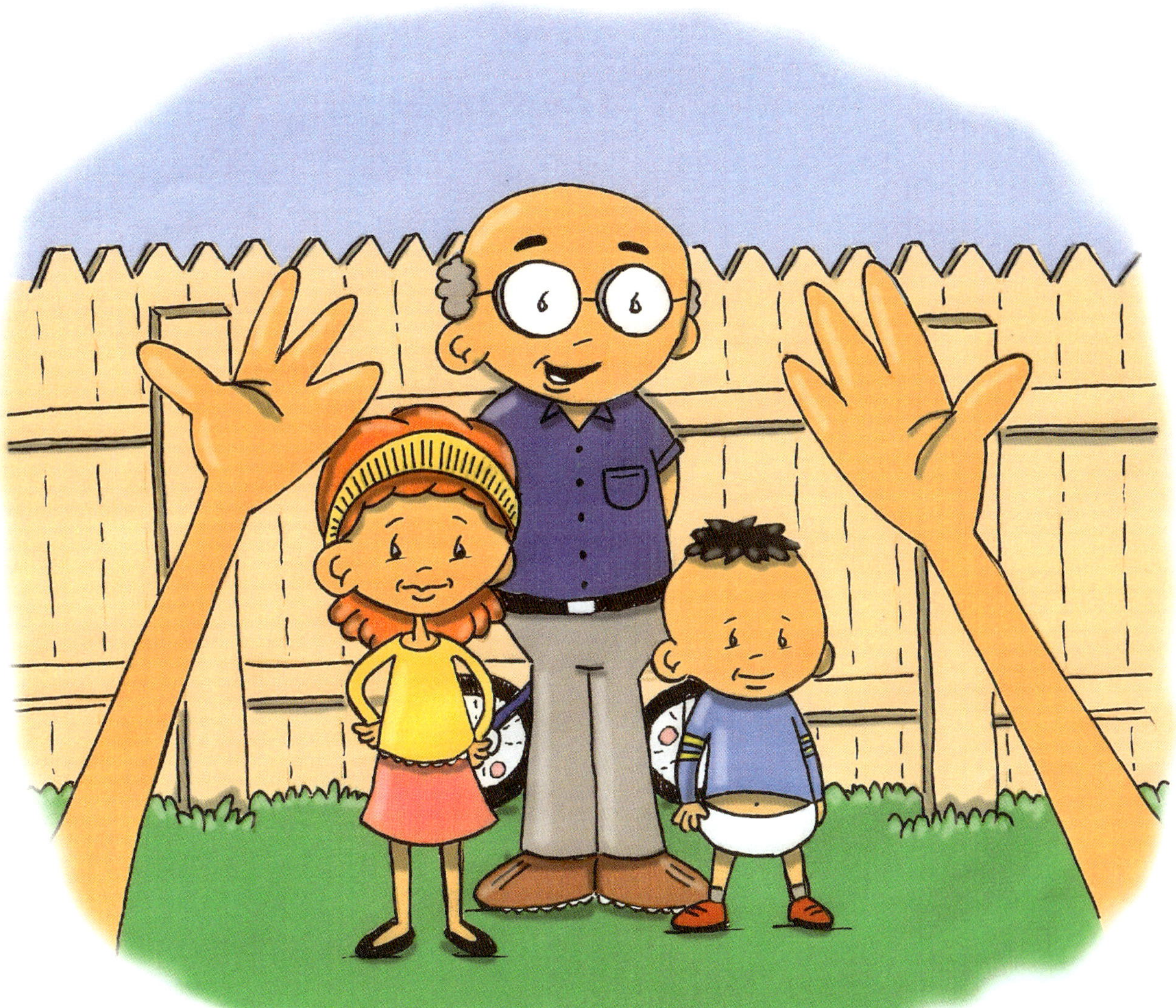

They've got smiles on their faces
"We've got something you'll like!"
Then they part in the middle
To reveal a new bike.

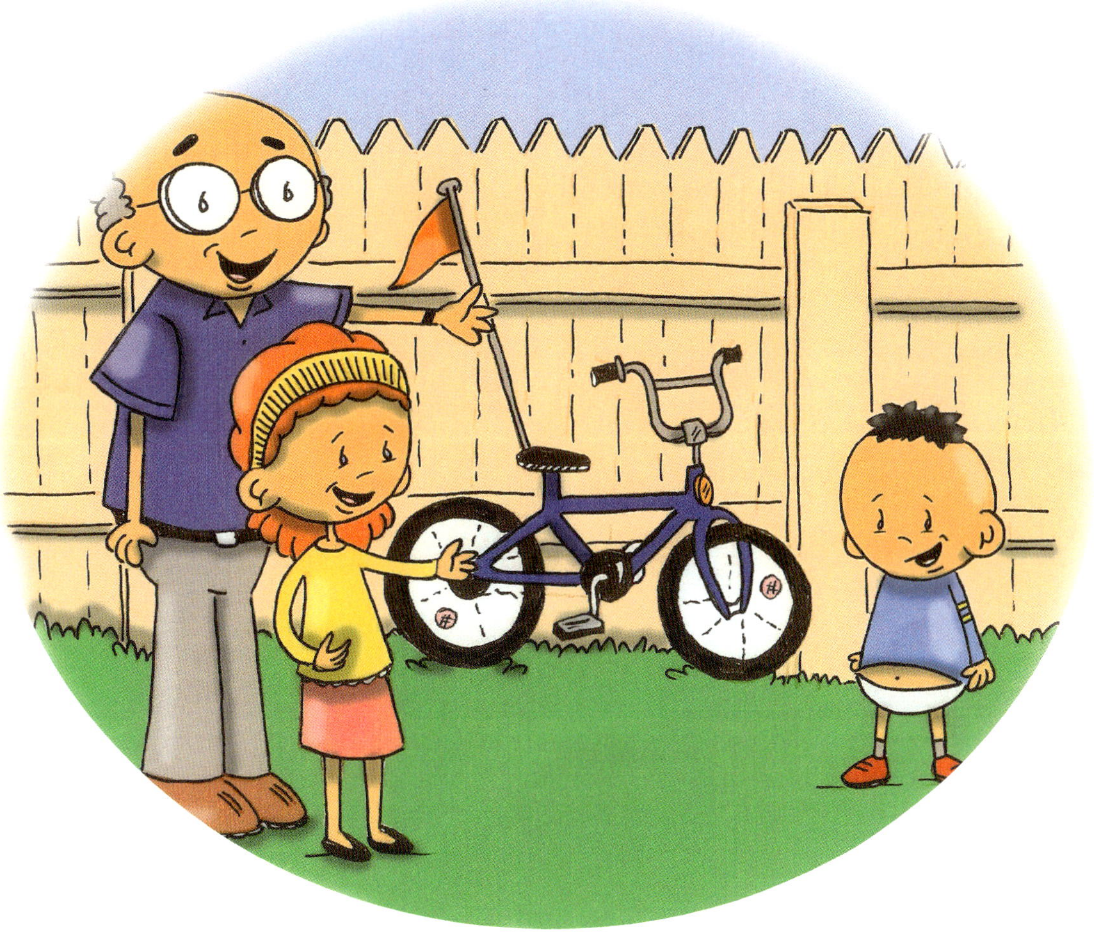

I run to my bike and shout
"Oh wow!" and "Oh man!"
"This bike is just awesome!
Thank you, thank you again!"

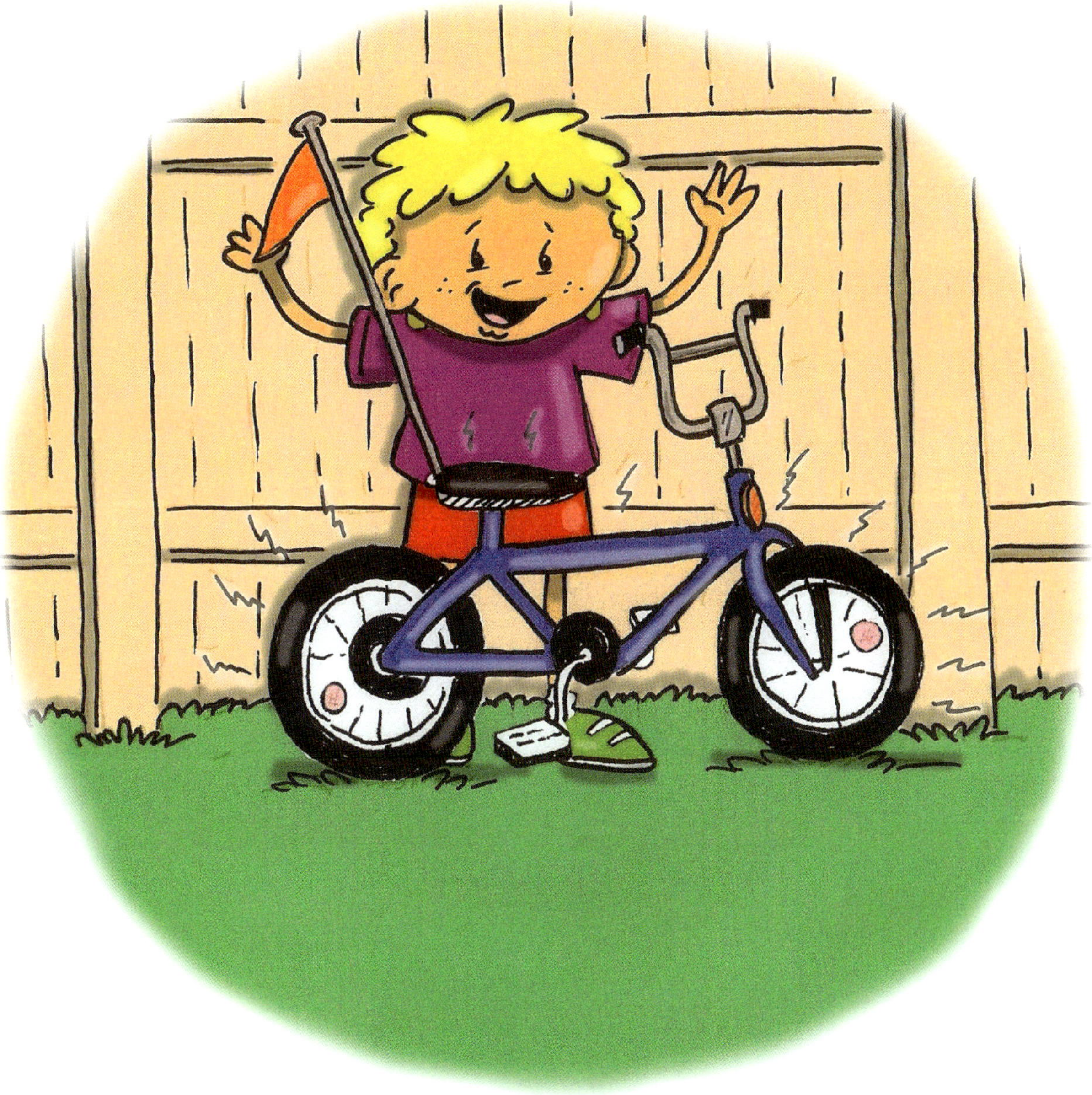

Mom gives me a helmet
To cover my head
And reties my laces
With double knots instead.

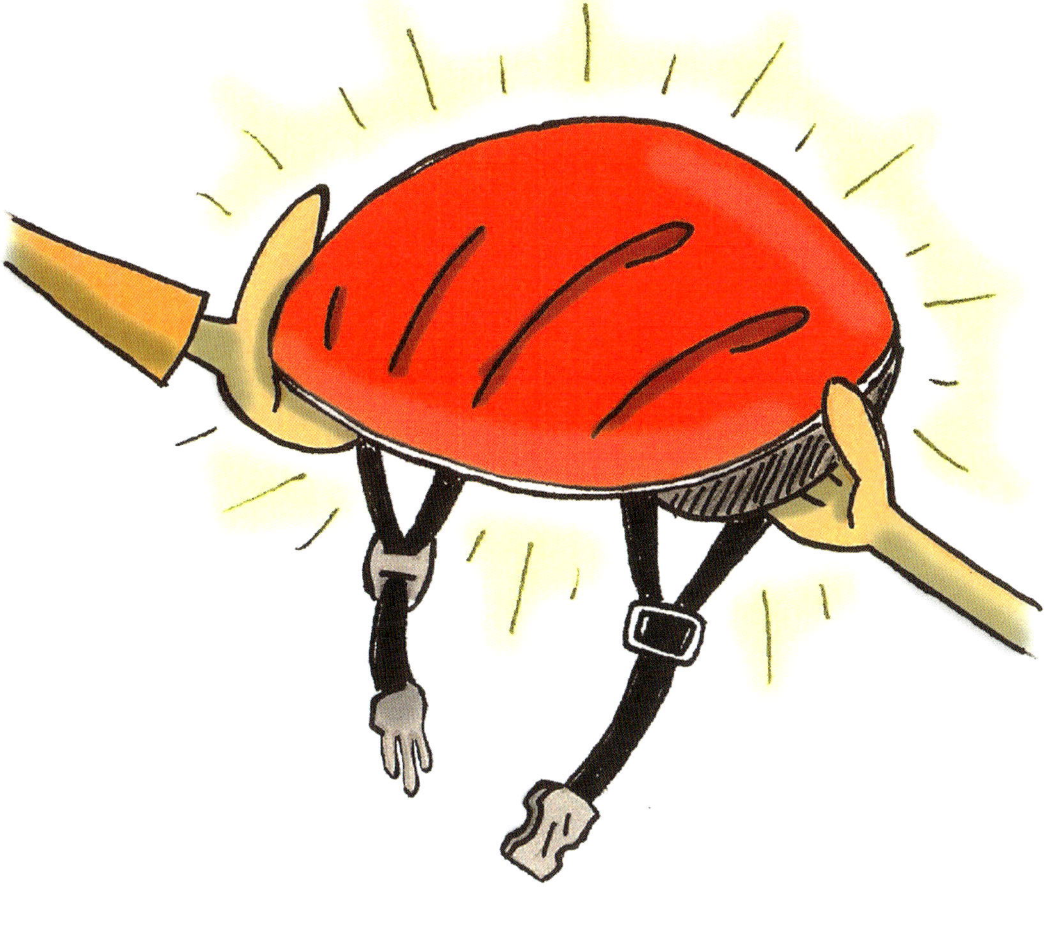

I straddle my legs
On each side of the bike
And center myself on the seat
For the flight.

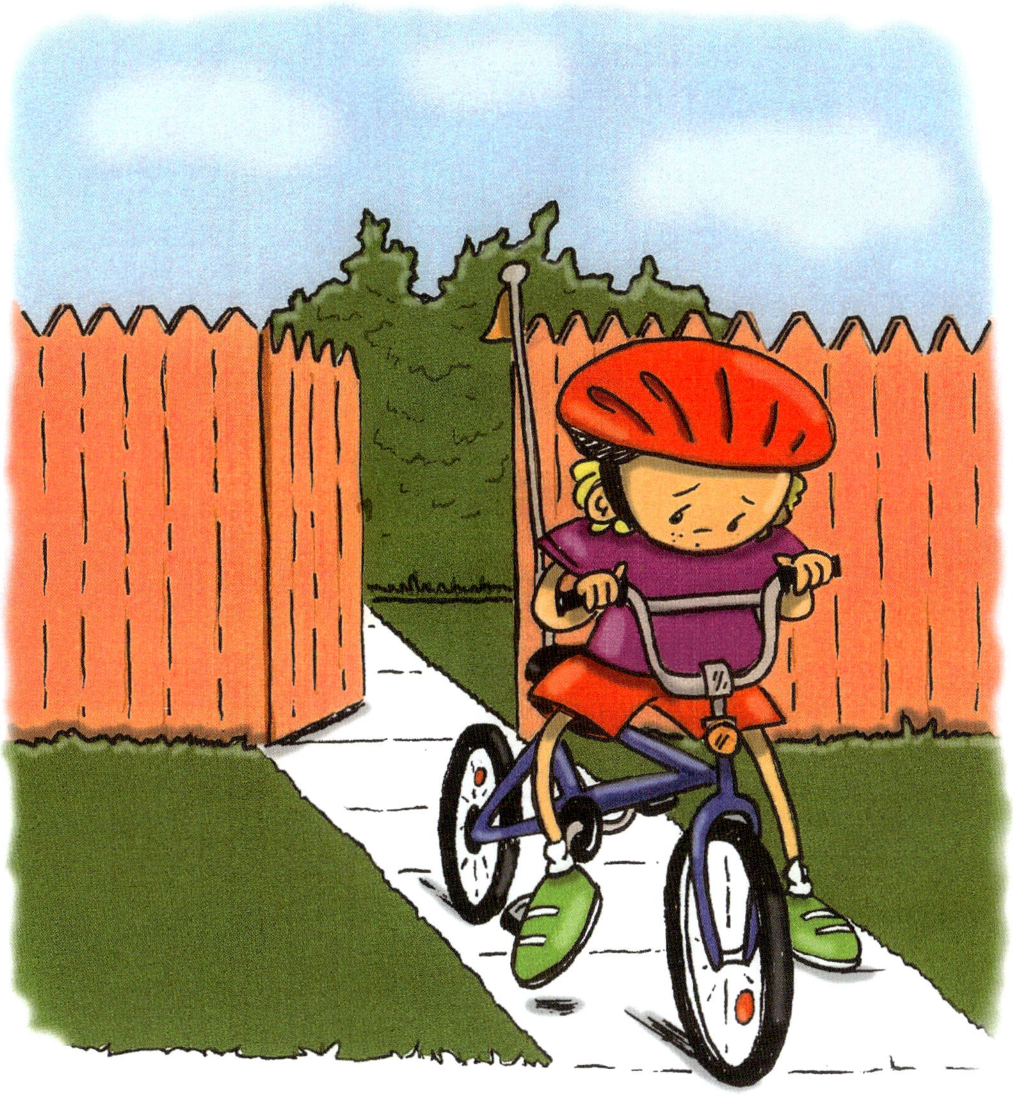

My toes touch the ground
But just barely I notice
So I look to my Grandpa
As I'm feeling quite nervous.

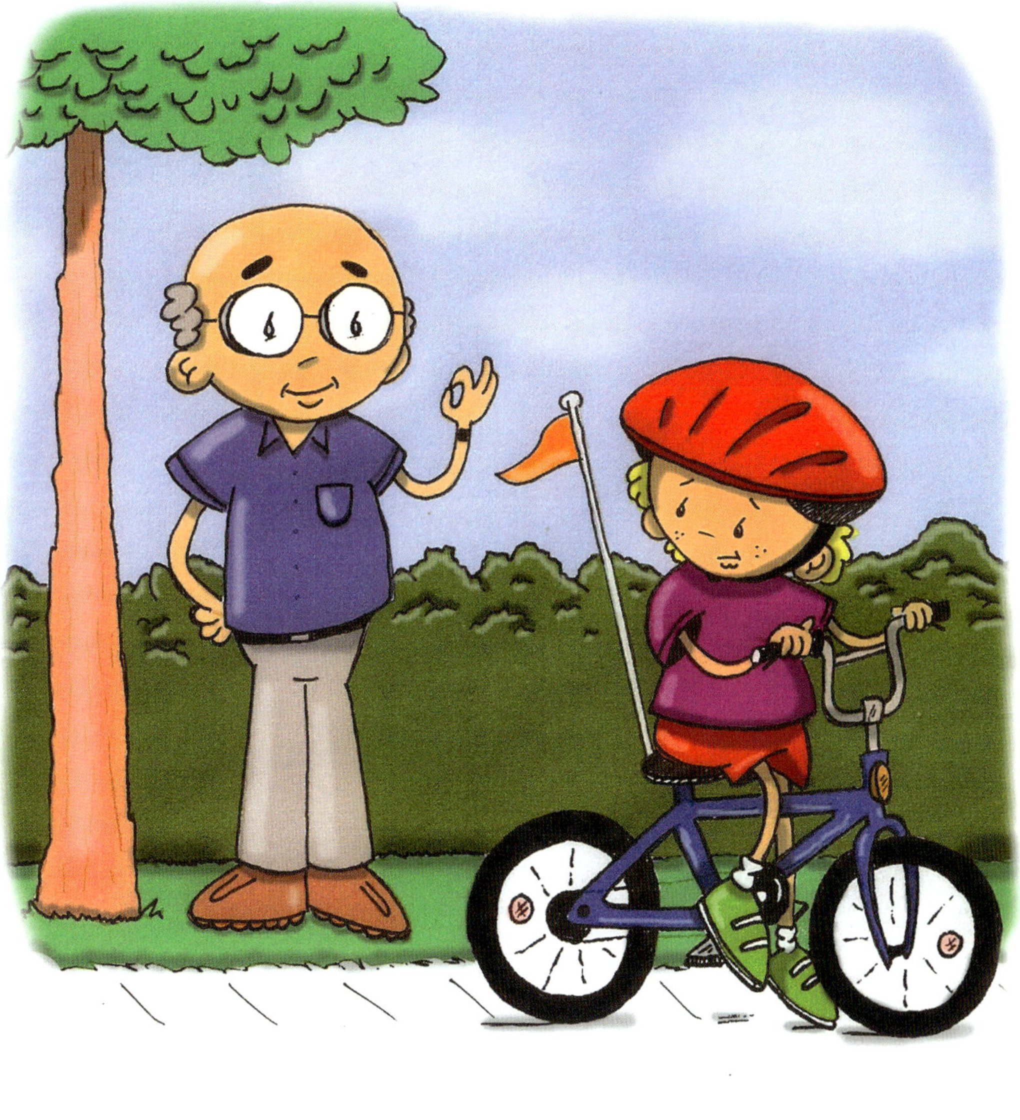

He smiles a wide grin
And comes over to help me
"Let's get started", he says
And pats my back gently.

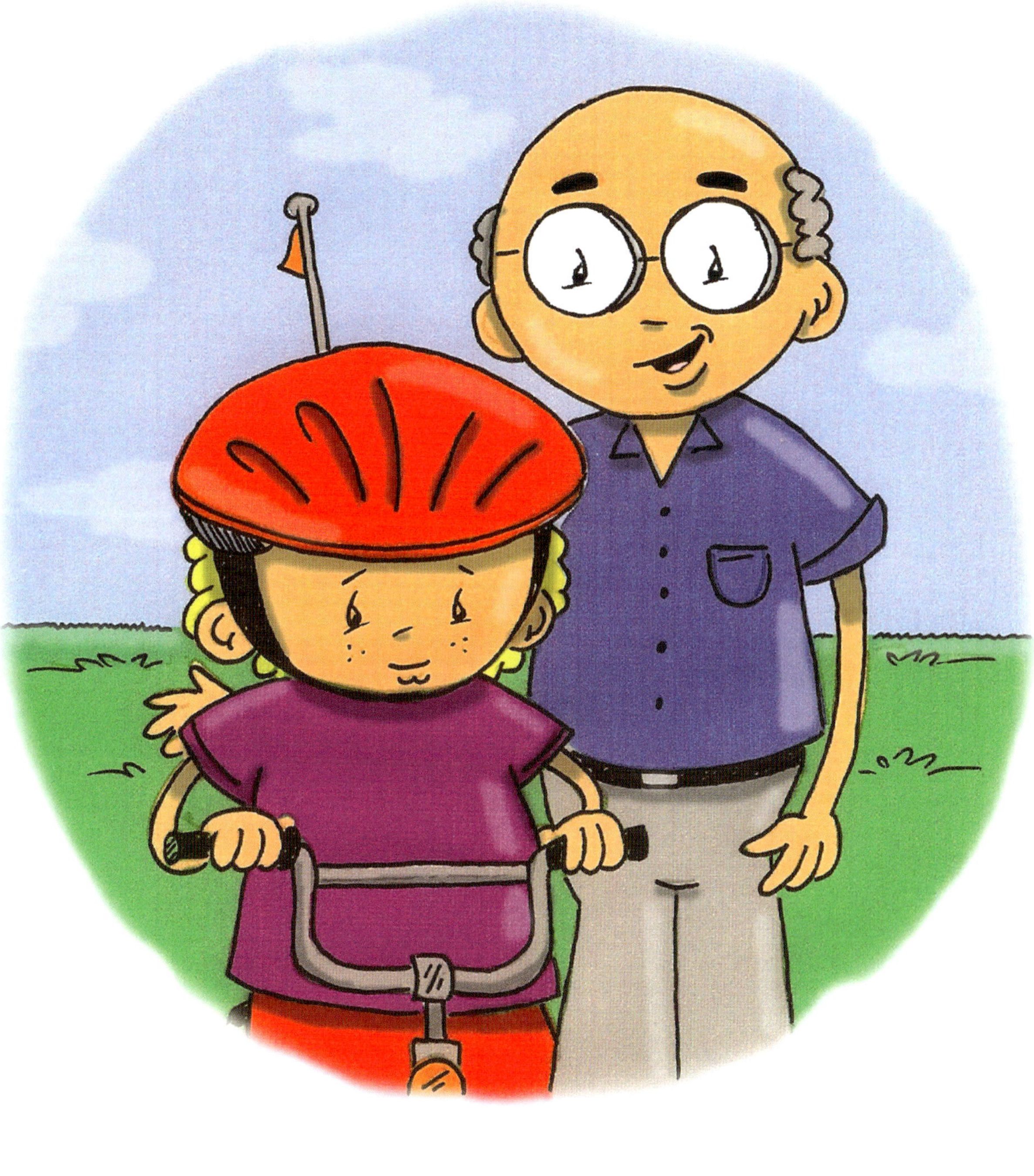

I gather my courage
Set one foot as I swallow
Then take a big breath
As my other foot follows.

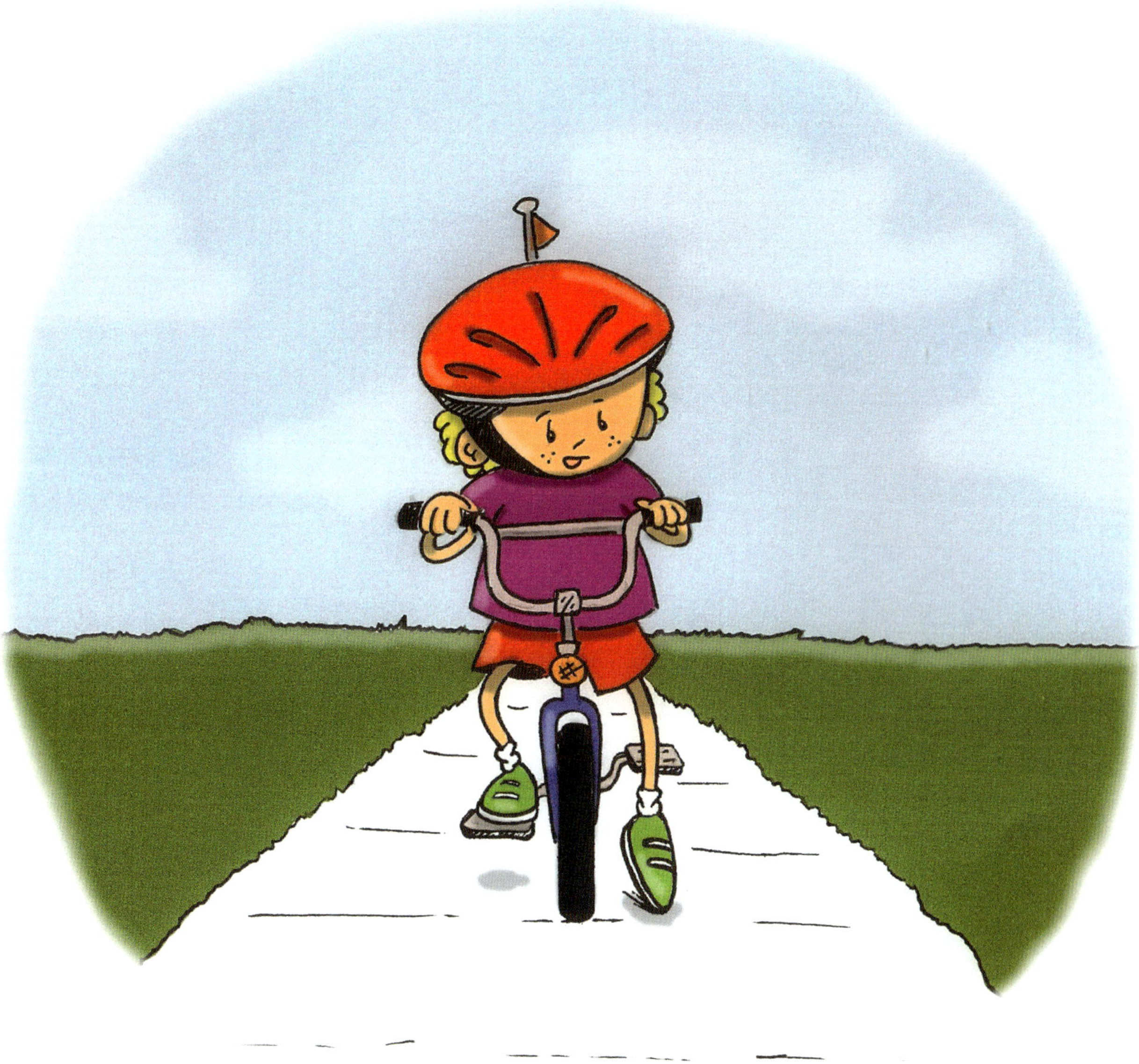

I'm a little bit wobbly
But my Grandpa says "Ready?"
Then he gives me a push
From the seat while I'm steady.

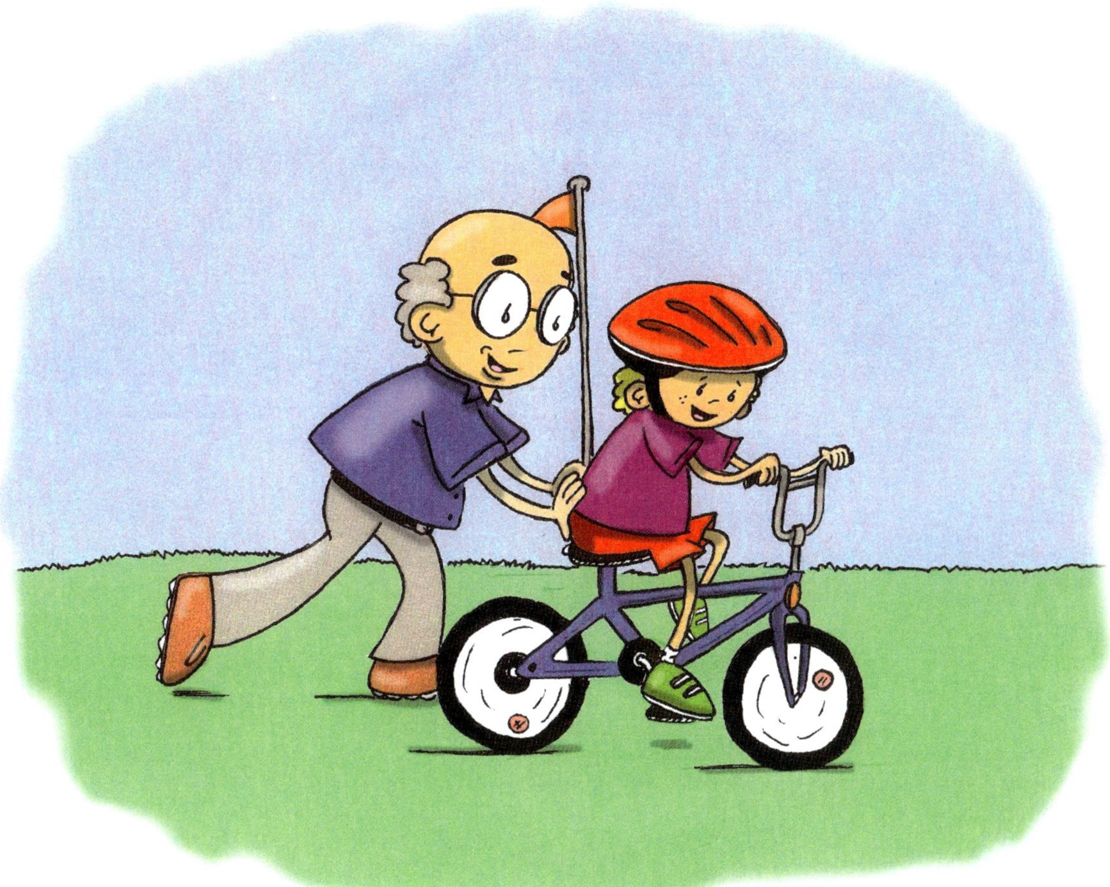

"Now pedal!" he shouts
And my family is cheering
"Sit up straight! Pedal faster!"
Is all I am hearing.

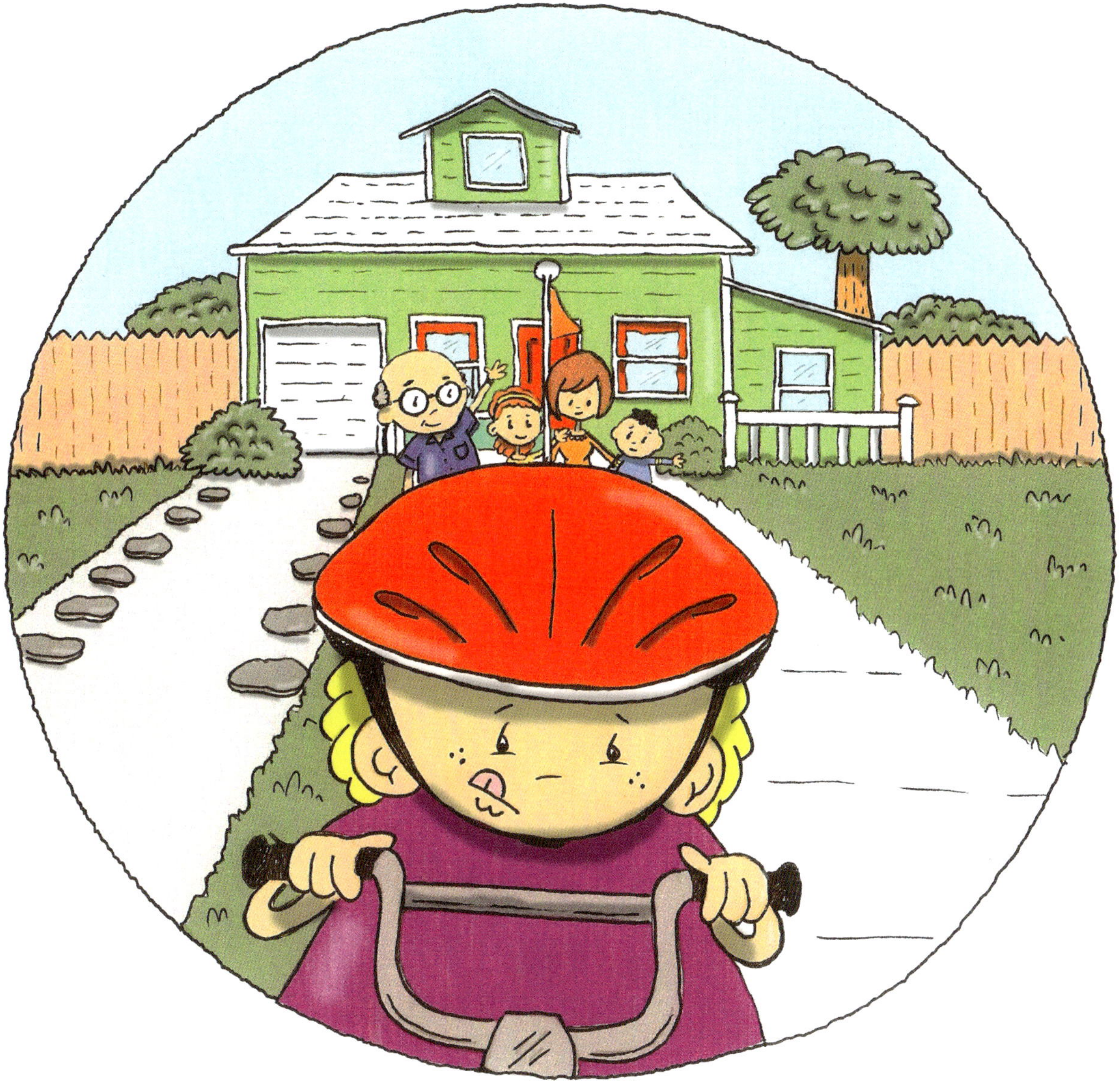

I guess that I fell
To one side or the other
But my feet were not far
From the ground I discovered.

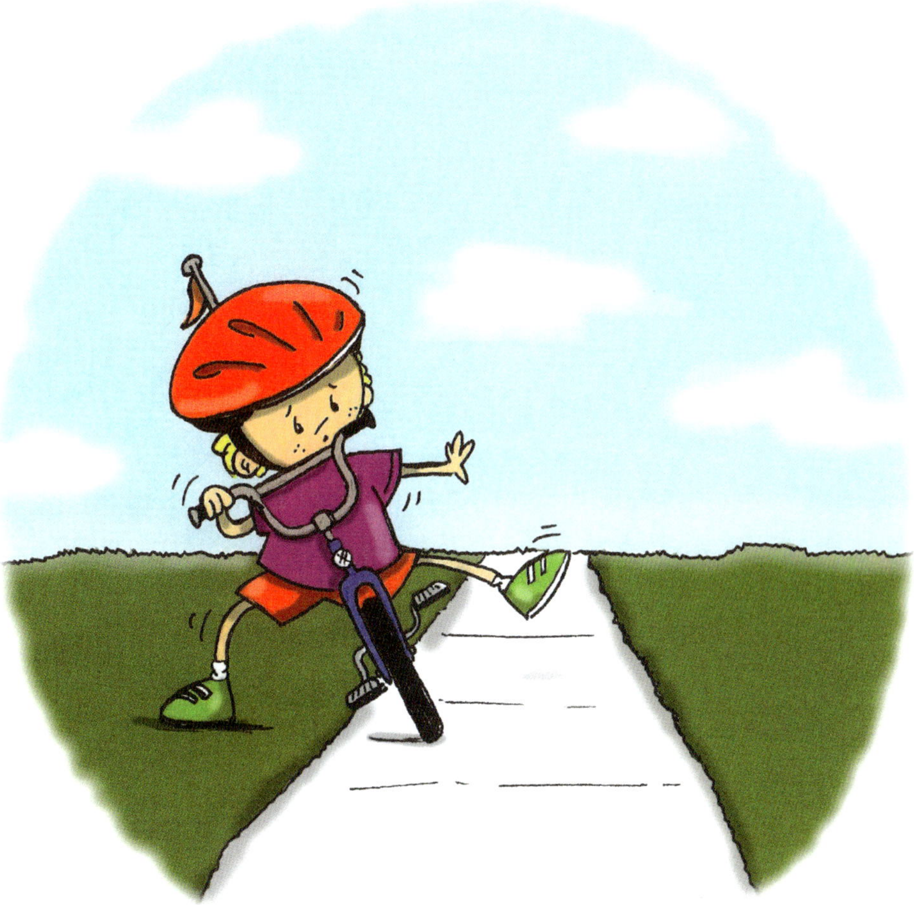

My family is clapping
And laughing and cheering.
(My Grandpa reminds me
To not forget steering.)

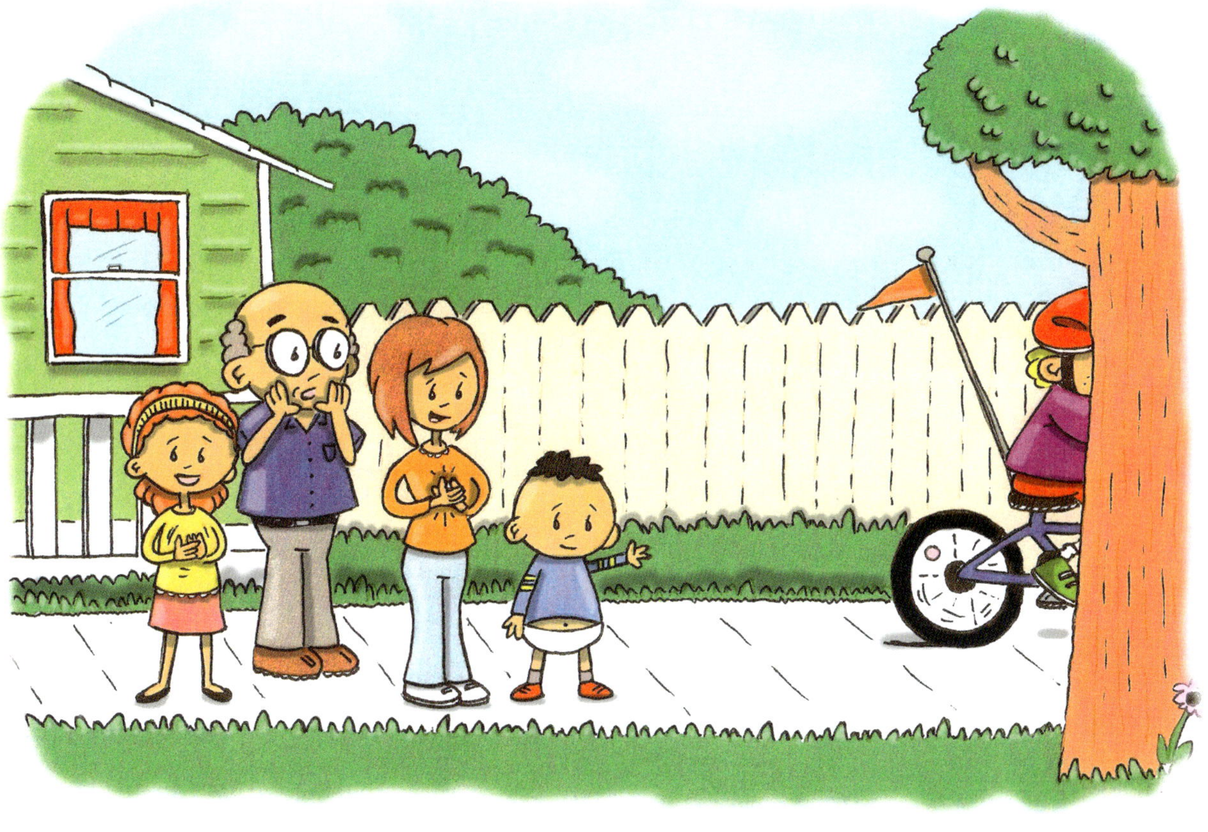

So I get myself straight
And sit back on the seat,
And promise myself
I will not see defeat.

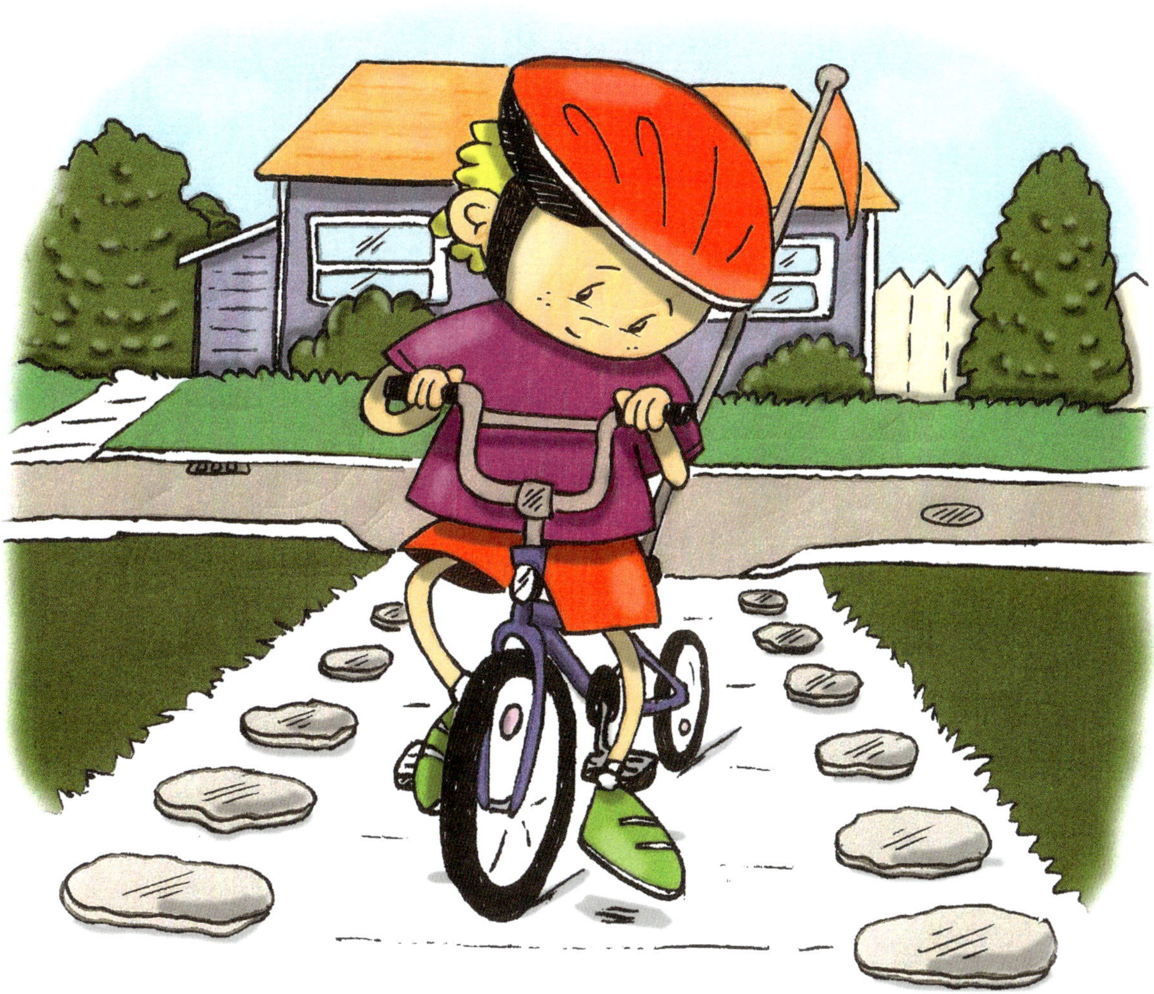

I've lifted one foot
Off the ground to that pedal
And start on my pep talk
As best as I'm able.

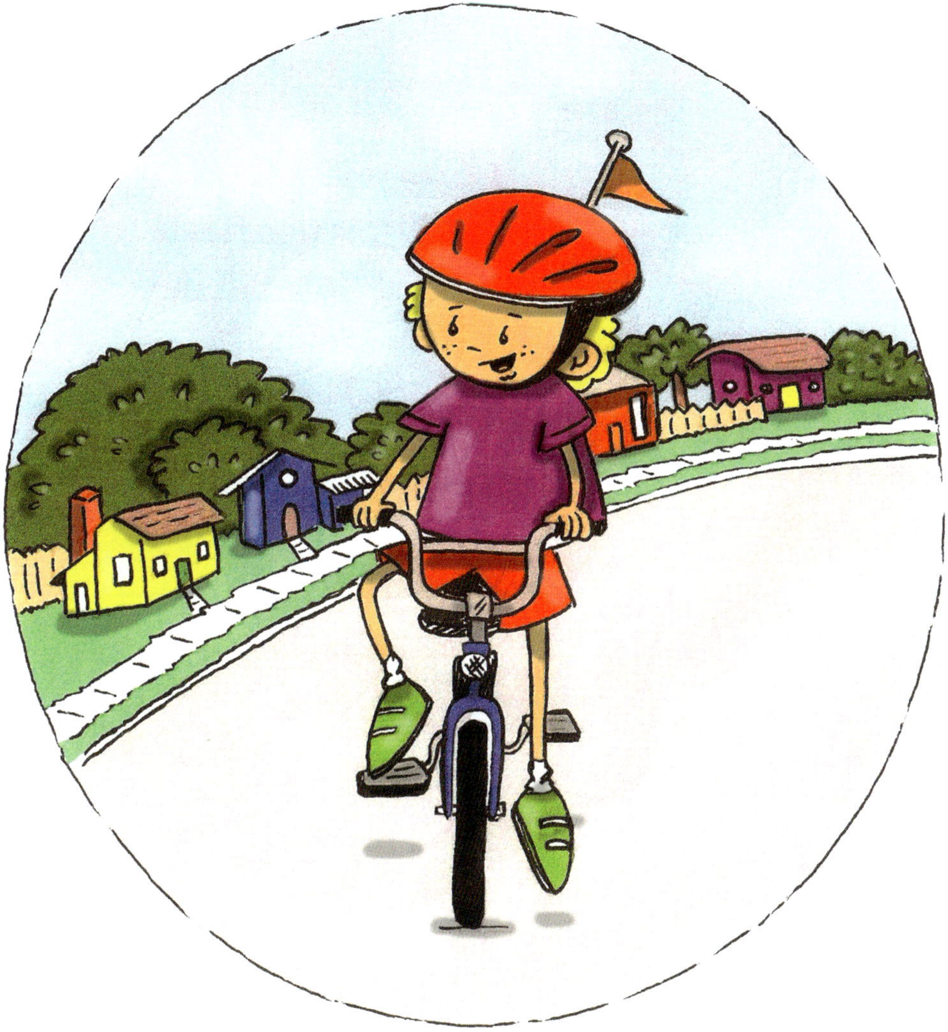

"You've watched all the other kids
Riding on by,
If they learned how to do it
You certainly must try."

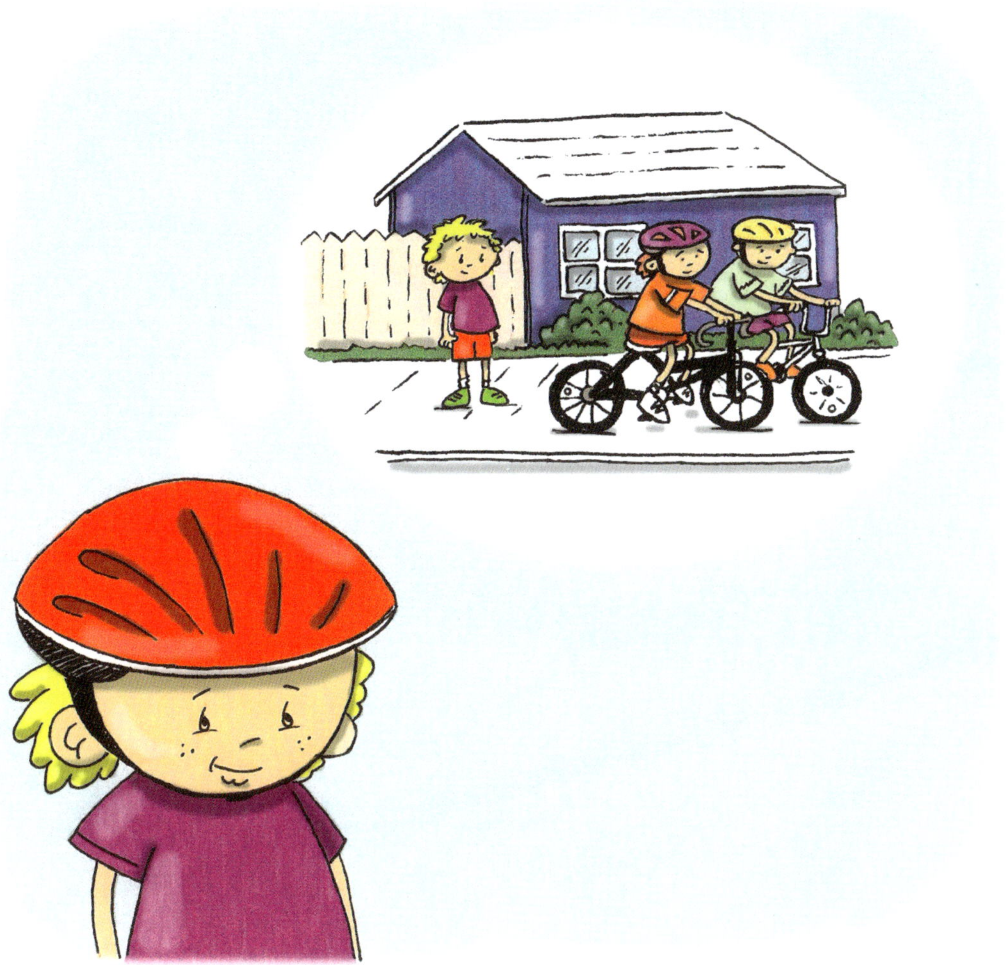

I think that I must have tried
Twenty-five times
Or fifty, or a hundred
To ride straight in a line.

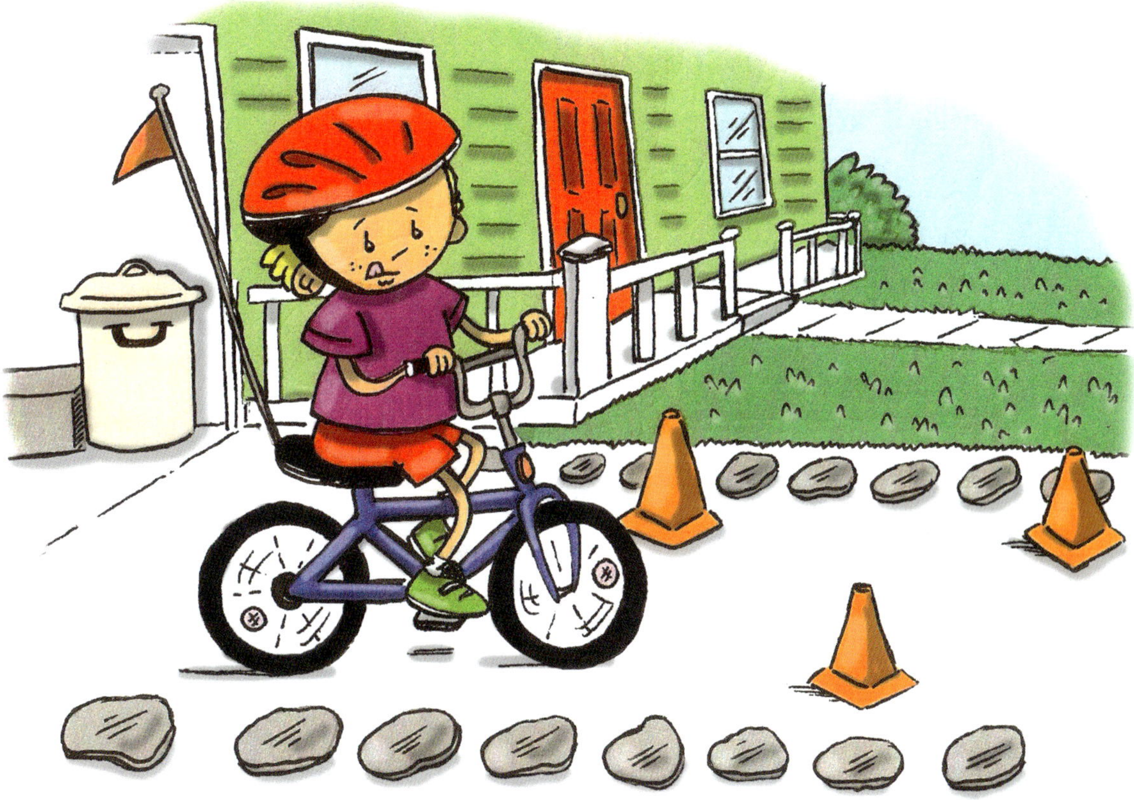

And finally I felt it
A bit more secure
My bike wobbled less
Practice was just the cure!

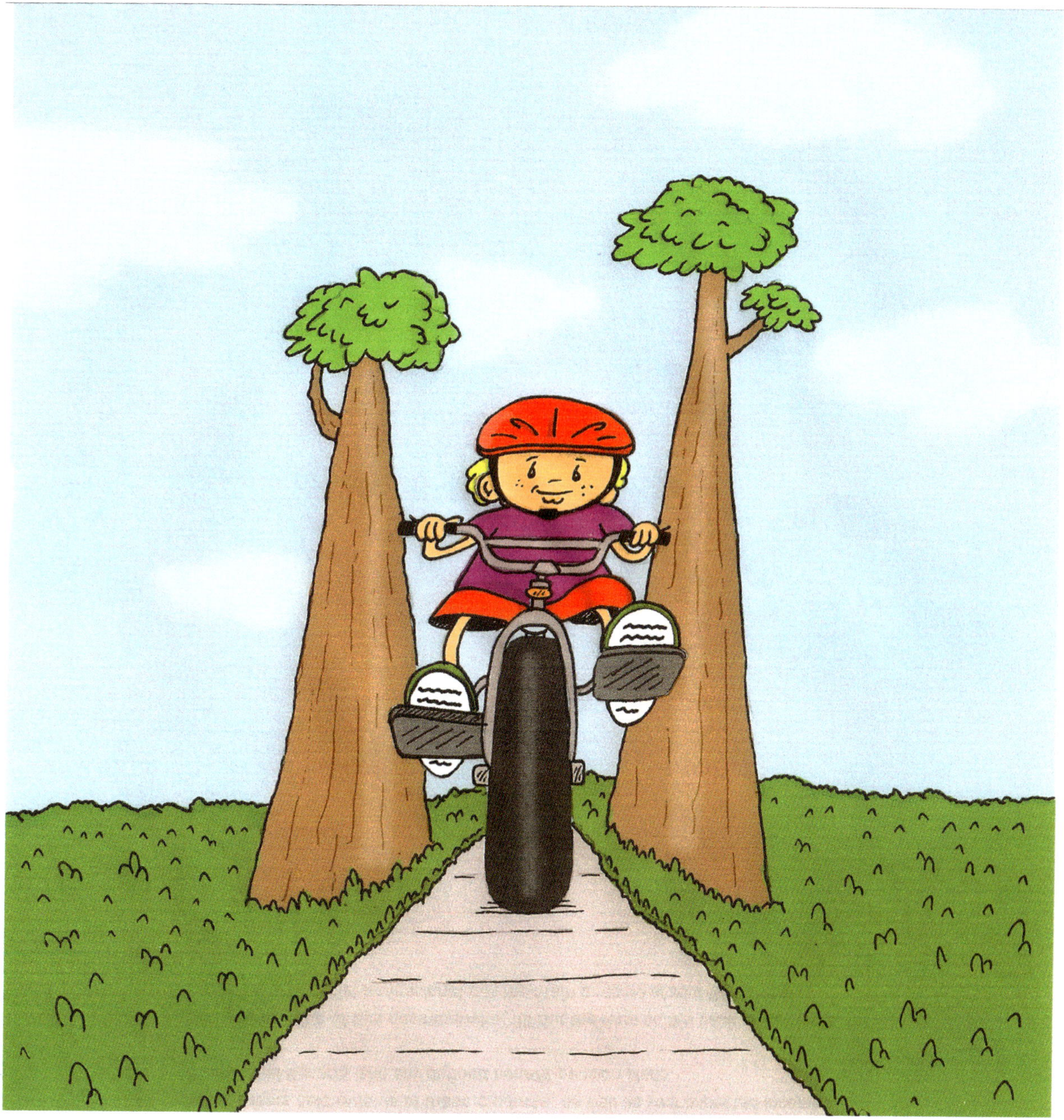

Everybody was cheering
As we went in for dinner.
I was learning to ride
And I felt like a winner!

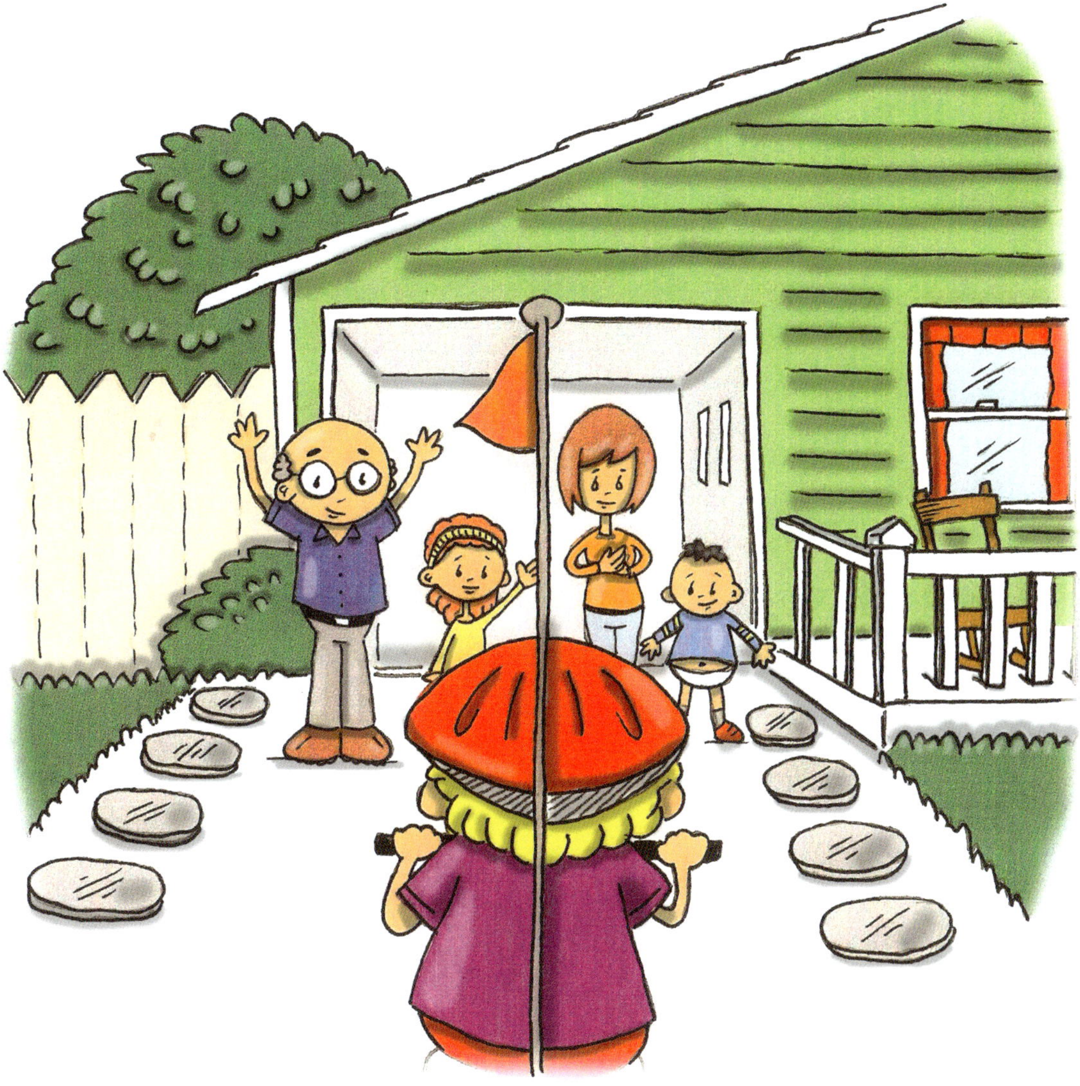

So I rode, and I rode
And I rode everyday.
I learned how to balance
And steer out of the way.

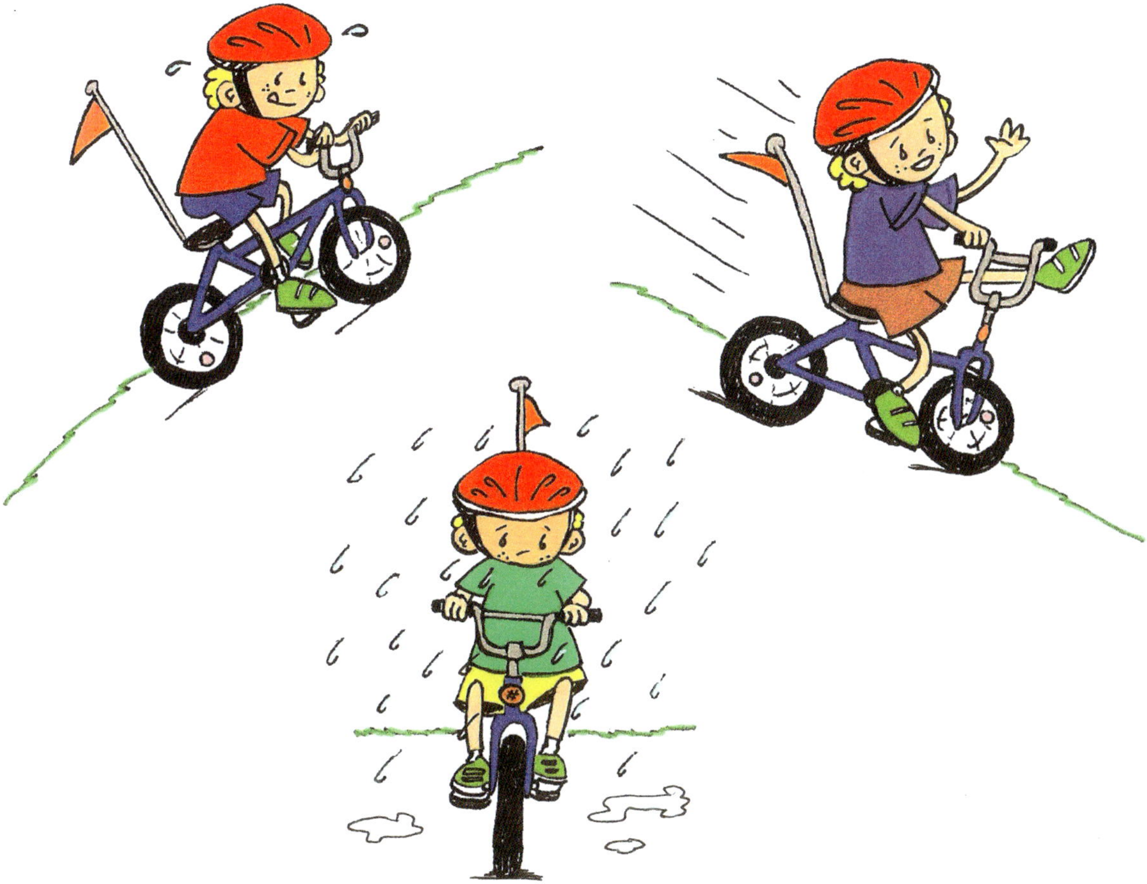

I rode from my driveway
And onto the walk
While mom and her friend
Sat on the porch as they talked.

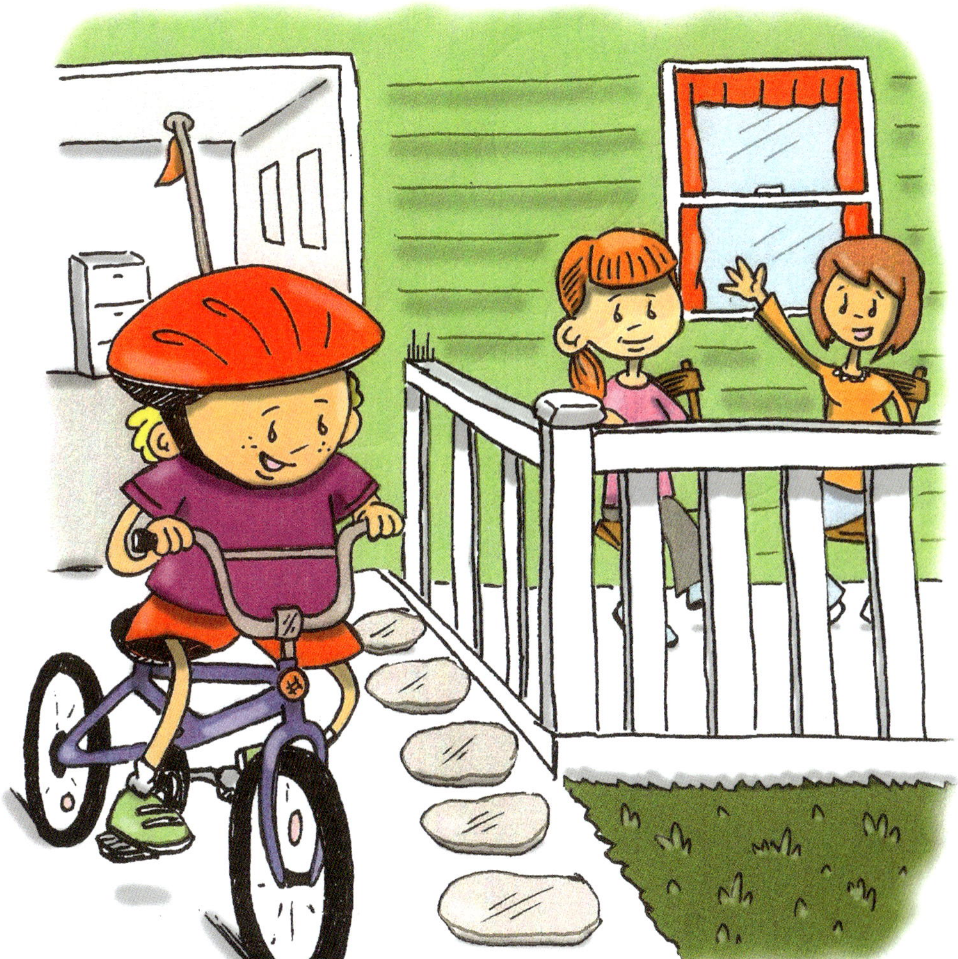

My driveway has cracks
On the side that is bumpy
Which bounces my voice
And it really sounds funny!

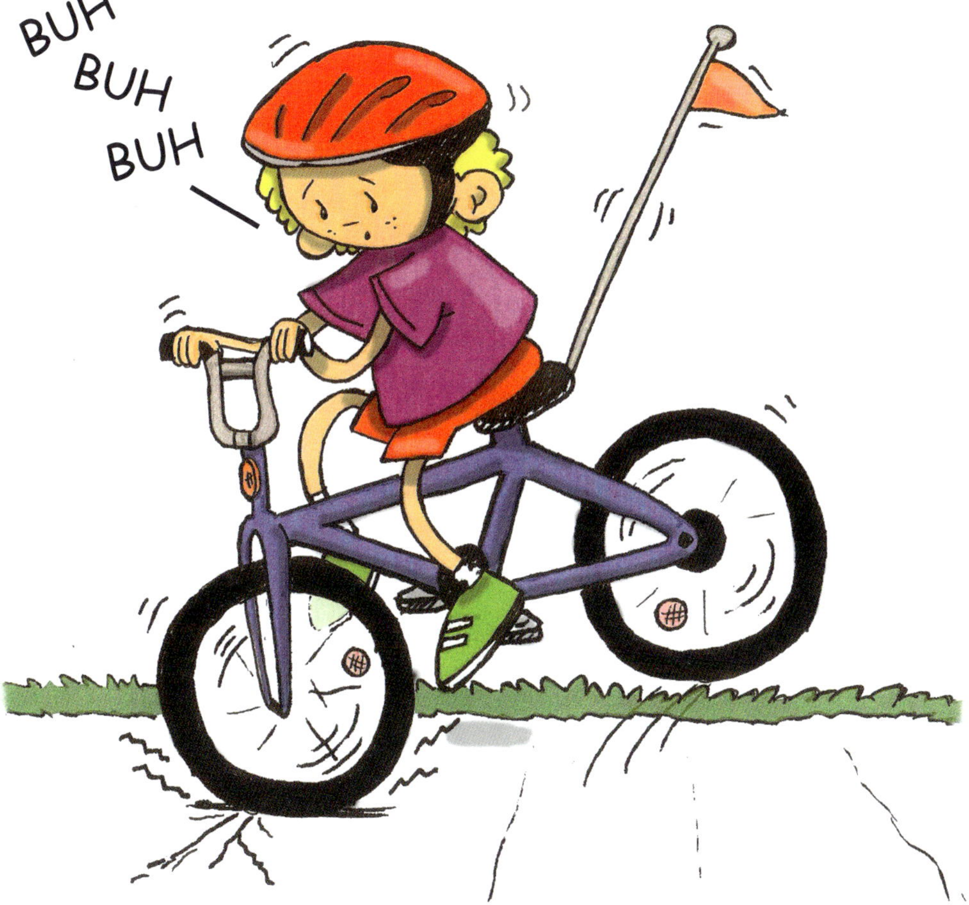
BUH
BUH
BUH

After the rain there are puddles
Of water and mud
So I ride right on through them
And get covered with crud!

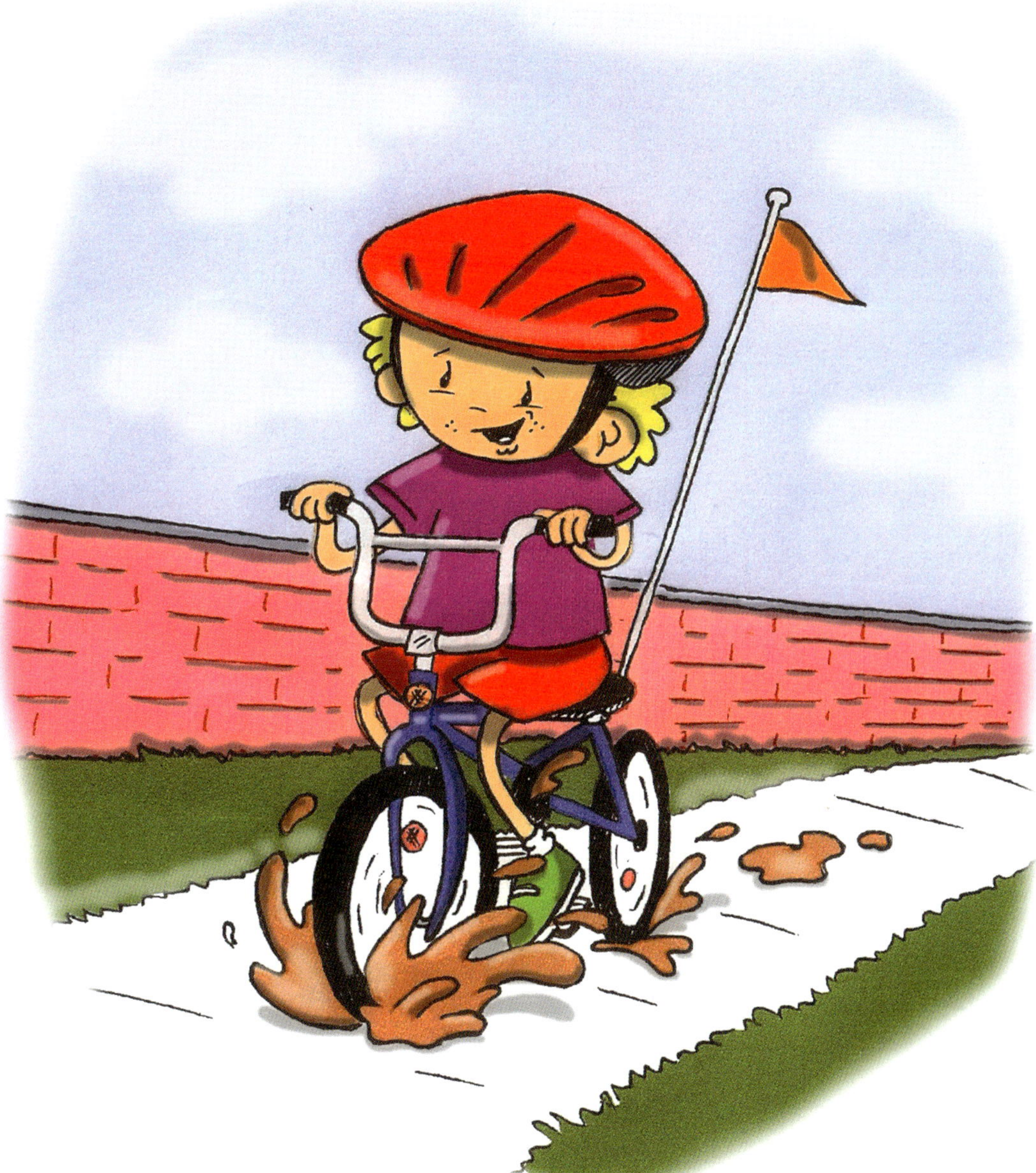

Sometimes my bike
Pedals faster than me
On a hill it's so fast
I lift my feet and shout..."WHEE!"

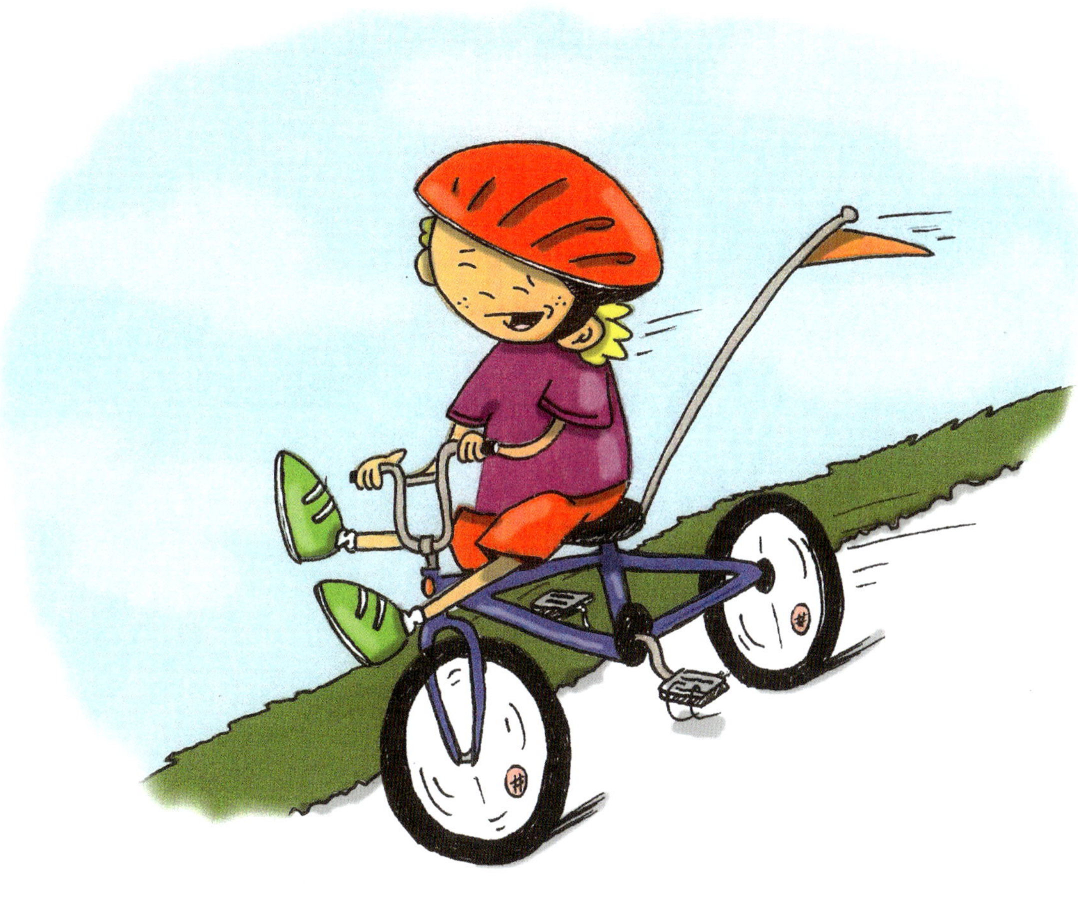

Once my dog chased my bike
Trying to nip at my feet
I wobbled and fell to the ground
Near the street.

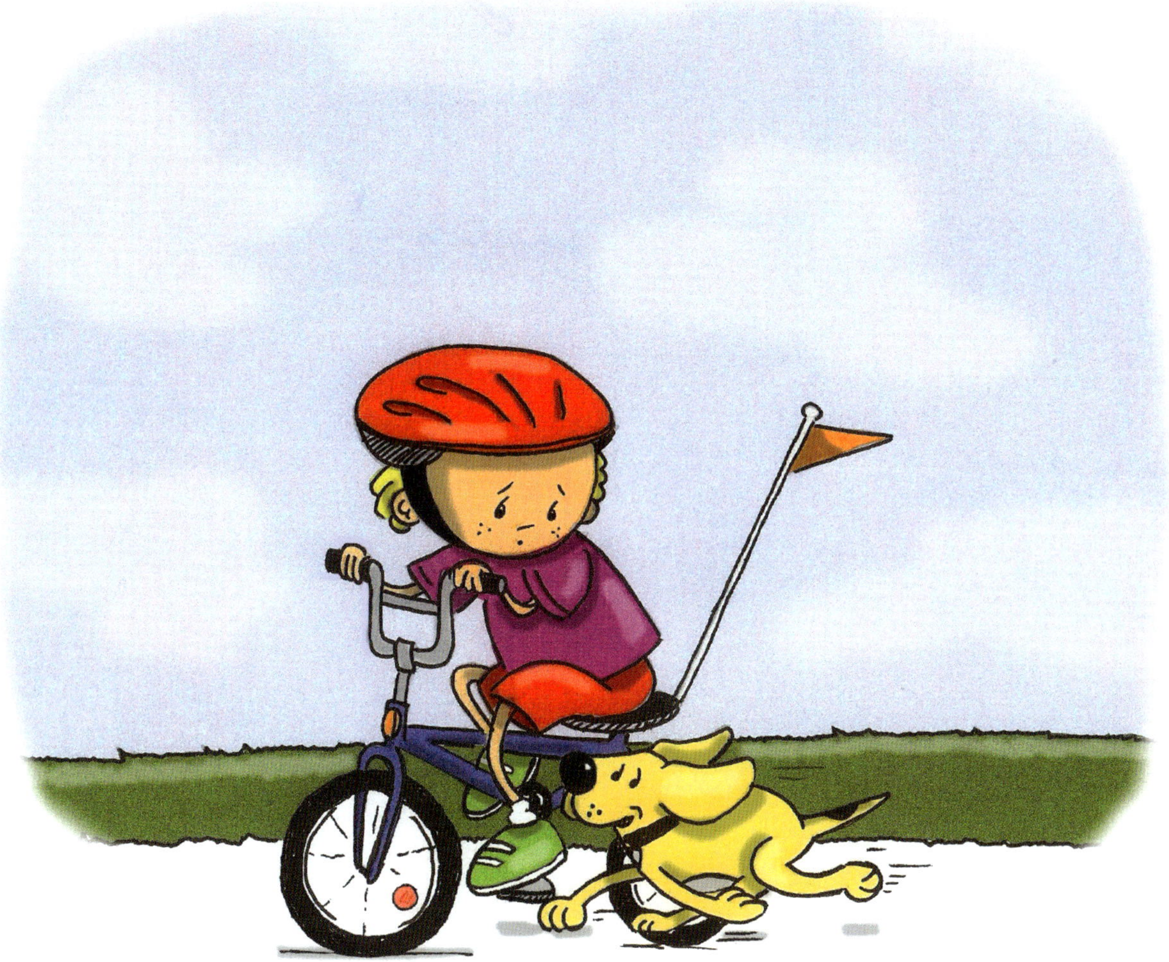

He gave me a lick
And then headed back home
While I wiped off the dirt
From my pants and the chrome.

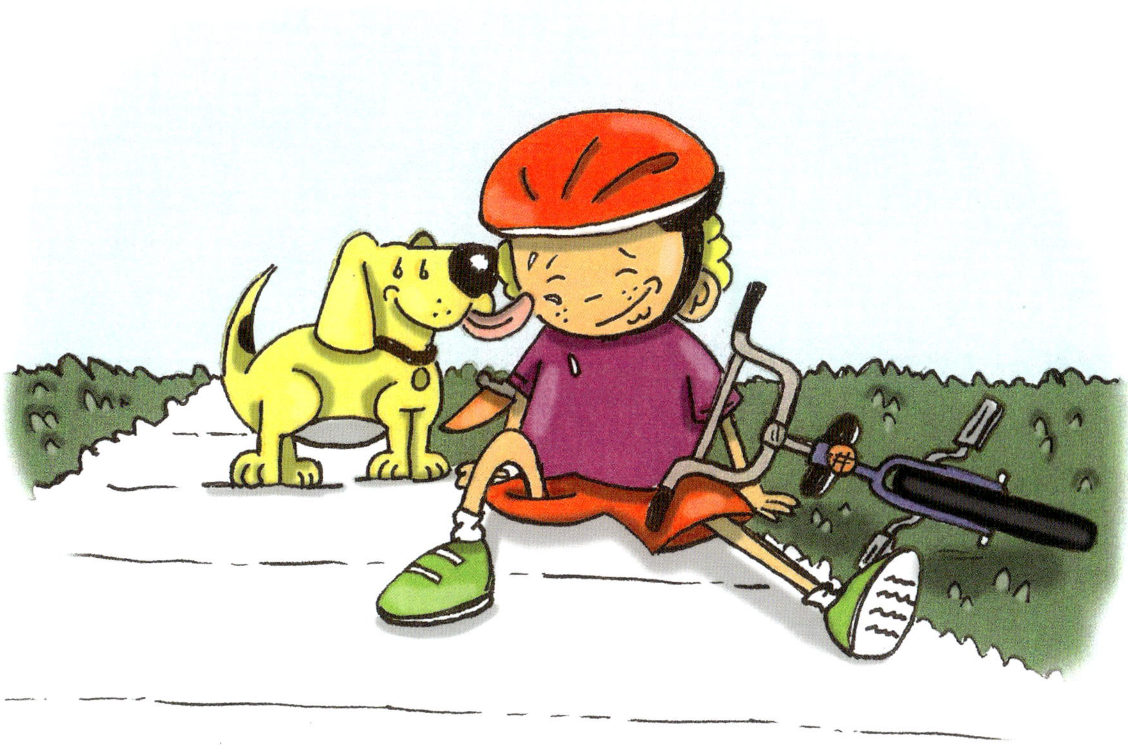

Now when I see that he's coming
I step up the pace
And lo and behold
I can win the dog race!

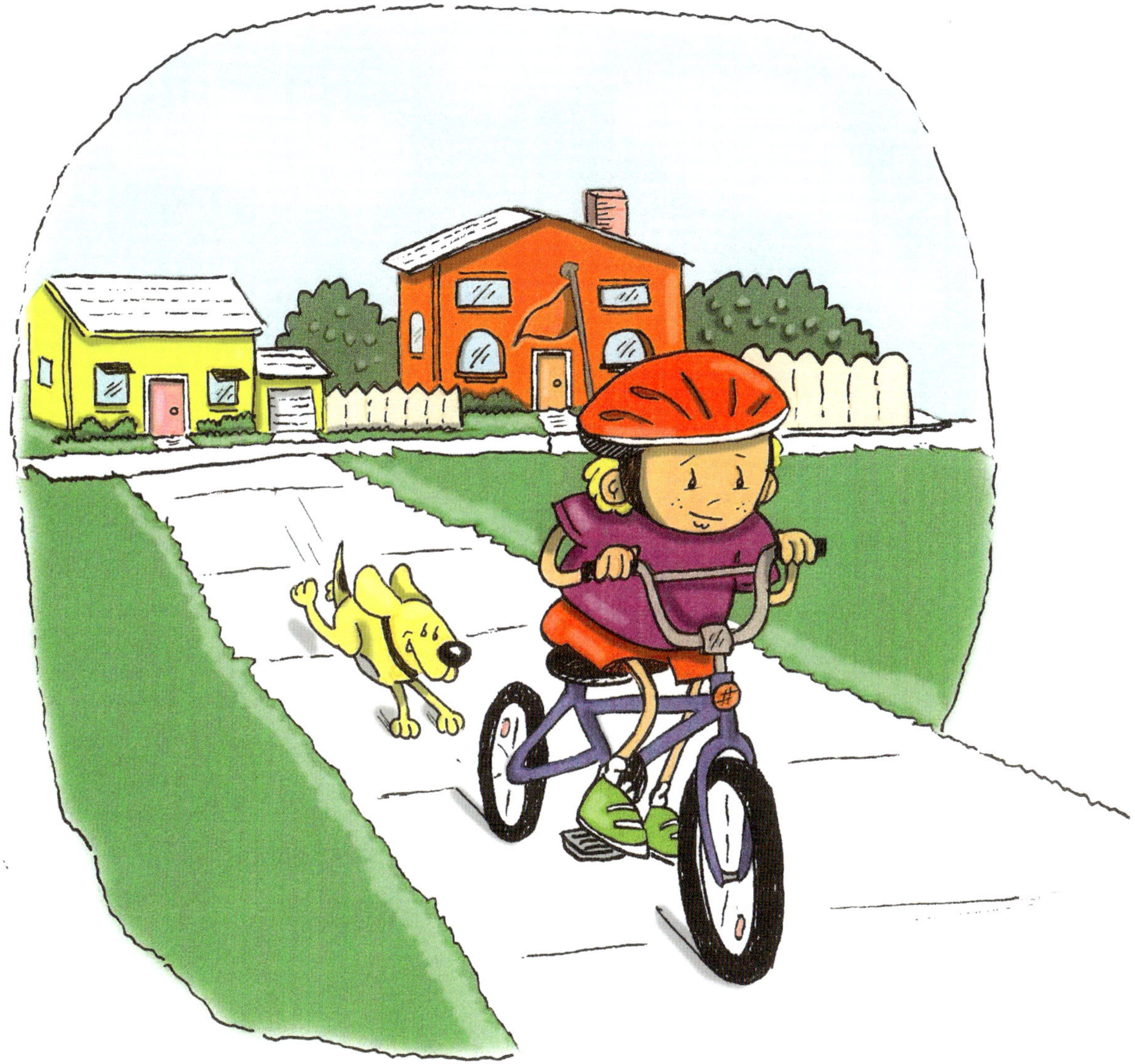

When I stand on the pedals
I can see for a mile
I'm tall and I'm cool
With a wind-plastered smile.

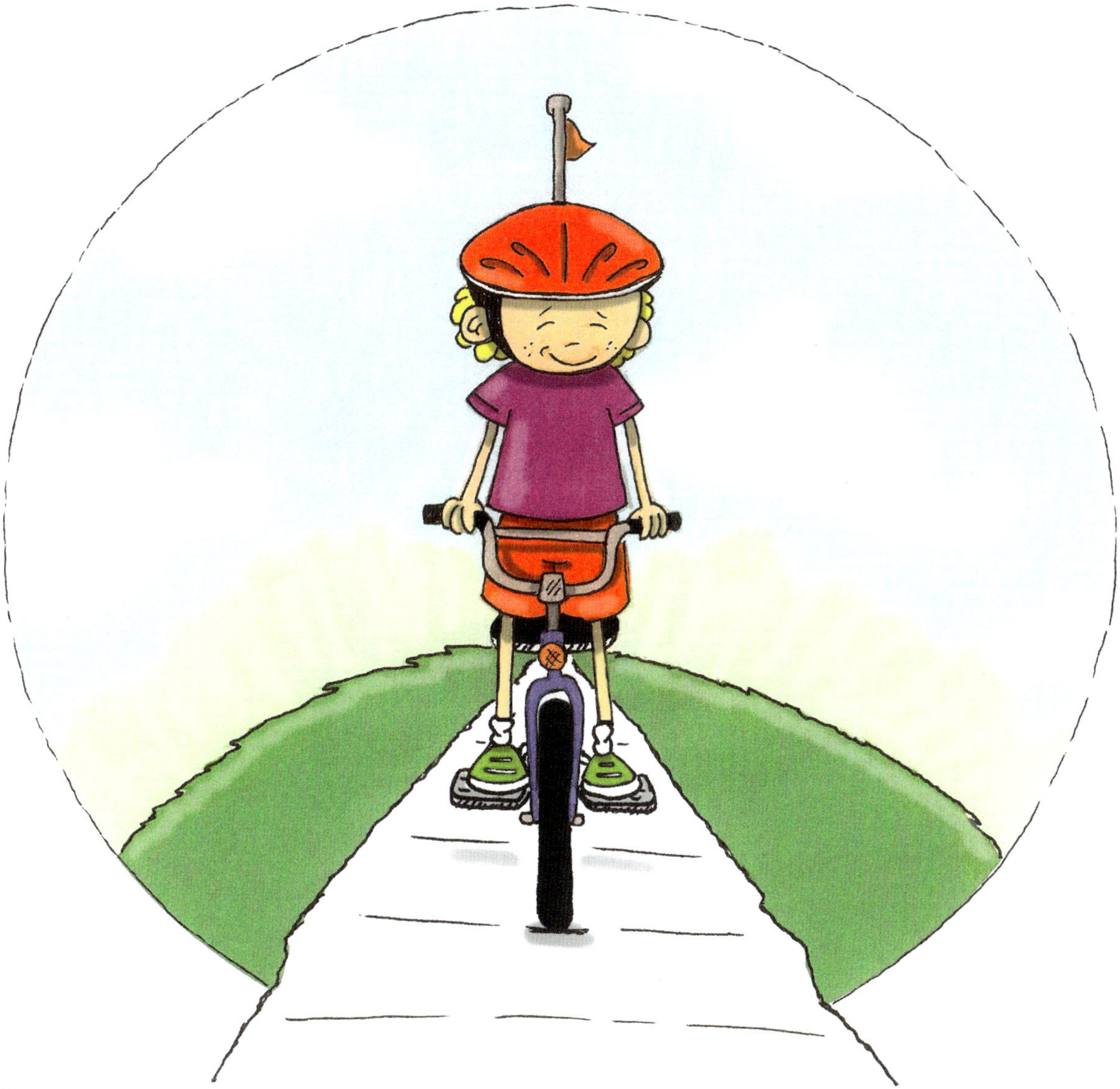

Now I'm off on my bike
And I whiz past the kids
And I watch as they watch me
Just like I once did.

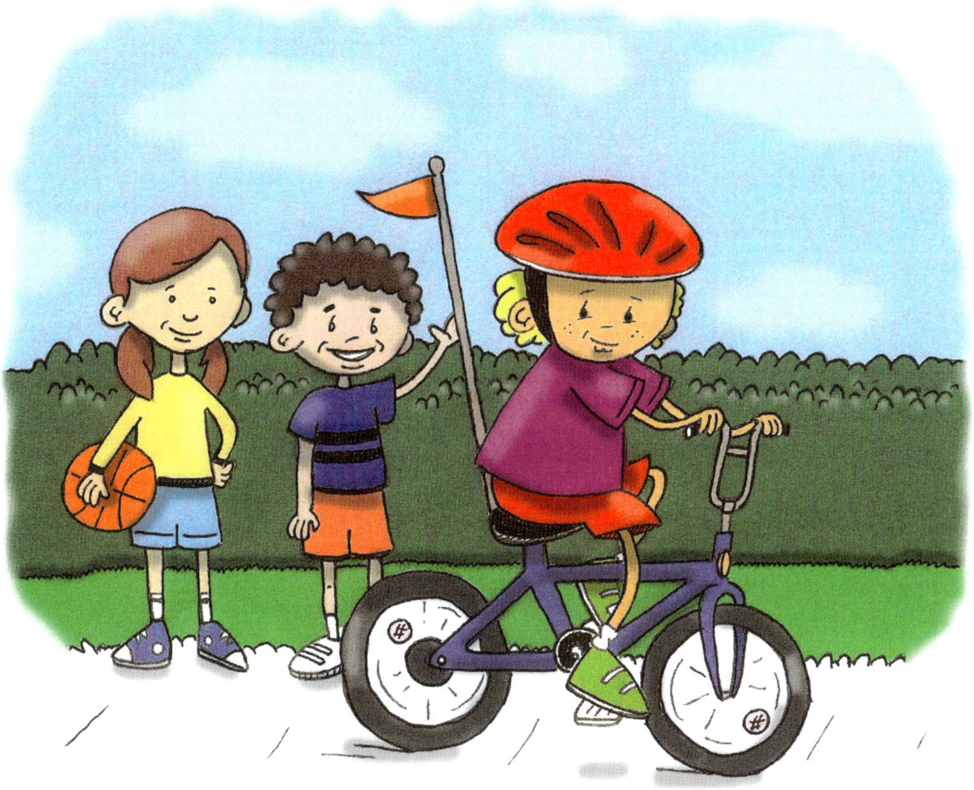

I love riding my bike
With the wind in my face
It's fun and it's fast
I'm a bike riding ace!

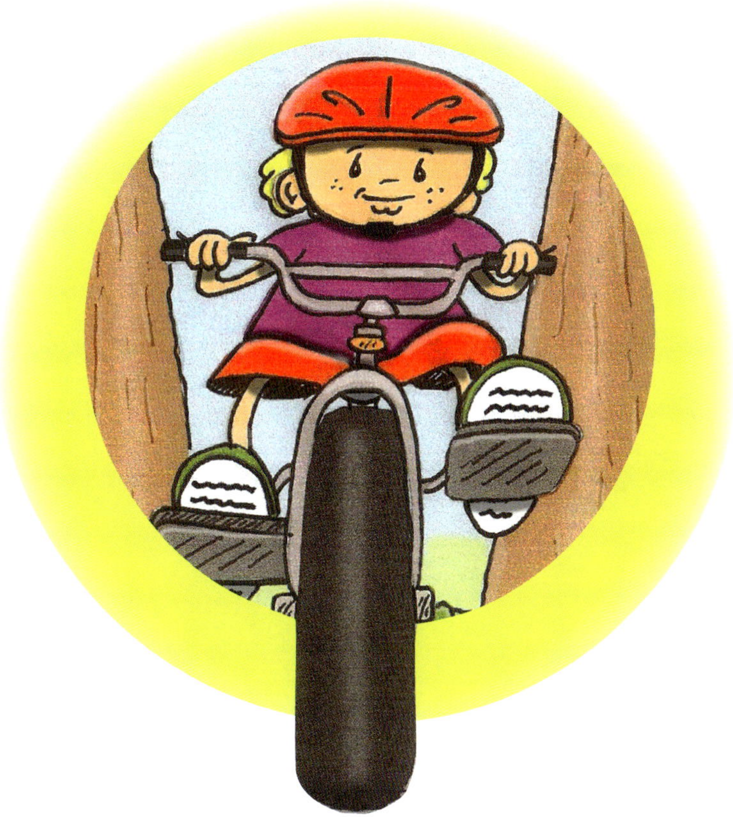

Story by Micheline Grace

Micheline Grace and her husband, Bob, reside near Des Moines, Iowa and are the parents of Katelyn and Jenna.

Her father wrote silly, rhyming poetry on all gift cards which made everything extra fun.

So, with that said...from Sidney to Micheline to you!

Photo by Janette Bradley Smith

Illustrations by Kevin Purcell

Kevin Purcell and his wife, Pam, live on Long Island with their 3 children, Ryan, Julia, and Sean.

Kevin began illustrating as a child, drawing caricatures of his friends and family. Some were flattered, others were not. Apologies to the latter.

Photo by Kornfeld Studios

Made in the USA
Charleston, SC
15 March 2010